For **John** - A. T. B.
For **Jago Bix** - A. A.

Let's
Dig and
Burrow

Please visit our web site at: **www.garethstevens.com**
For a free color catalog describing Gareth Stevens' list of high-quality books and
multimedia programs, call 1-800-542-2595 (USA) or 1-800-461-9120 (Canada).
Gareth Stevens Publishing's Fax: (414) 332-3567.

Library of Congress Cataloging-in-Publication Data

Nilsen, Anna, 1948-
    Let's dig and burrow / written by Anna Nilsen; illustrated by Anni Axworthy.
      p. cm. – (Animal antics)
    ISBN 0-8368-2910-7 (lib. bdg.)
    1. Animal behavior–Juvenile literature. [1. Animals–Habits and behavior.]
  I. Axworthy, Anni, ill. II. Title.
  QL756.15.N56 2001
  590–dc21   2001020885

This North American edition first published in 2001 by
Gareth Stevens Publishing
A World Almanac Education Group Company
330 West Olive Street, Suite 100
Milwaukee, WI 53212 USA

Gareth Stevens editor: Dorothy L. Gibbs
Cover design: Tammy Gruenewald

This edition © 2001 by Gareth Stevens, Inc. First published by Zero to Ten Limited, a member of the
Evans Publishing Group, 327 High Street, Slough, Berkshire SL1 1TX, United Kingdom. © 1999 by Zero
to Ten Ltd. Text © 1999 by Anna Nilsen. Illustrations © 1999 by Anni Axworthy. This U.S. edition
published under license from Zero to Ten Limited.

Printed in the United States of America

1 2 3 4 5 6 7 8 9 05 04 03 02 01

Let's
Dig and
Burrow

Written by
Anna Nilsen

Illustrated by
Anni Axworthy

Gareth Stevens Publishing
A WORLD ALMANAC EDUCATION GROUP COMPANY

Moles
make a
mess
when they

dig
and
burrow.

To keep cool
when it's hot,
little lizards

dig
and
burrow.

When chipmunks
store their food,
they chip and
chatter as they

dig
and
burrow.

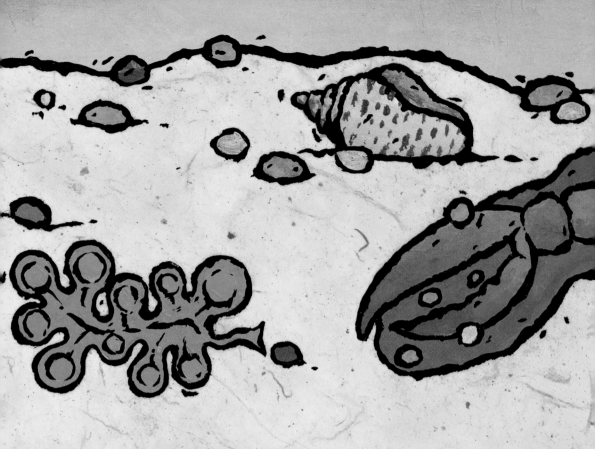

Some
crabs will
die if
they don't

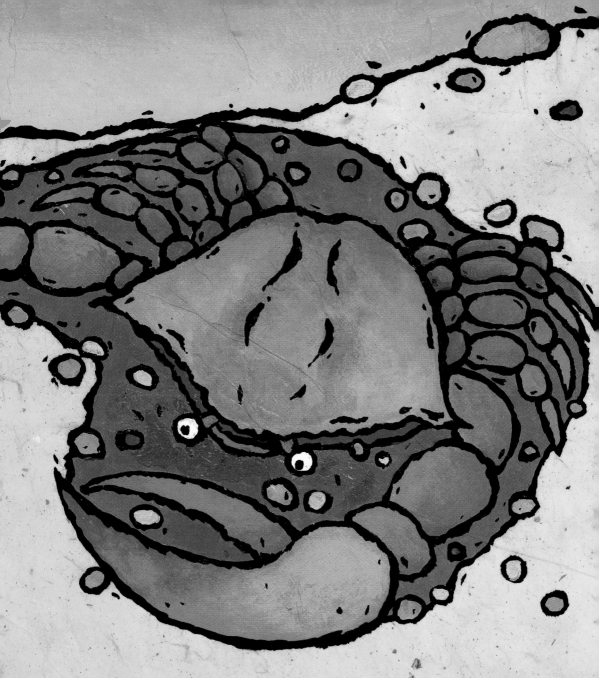

dig
and
burrow.

Rabbits, beware!
Hungry foxes
also like to

dig
and
burrow.

Especially
when it rains,
in the soft and
squelchy soil,

squiggly, wriggly
worms just love to

dig
and
burrow.

To make nests
for their young,
meerkats always

dig
and
burrow.

When dogs bury
treats, they have to

dig
and
burrow.

Even boys and
girls like you
sometimes

dig
and
burrow.